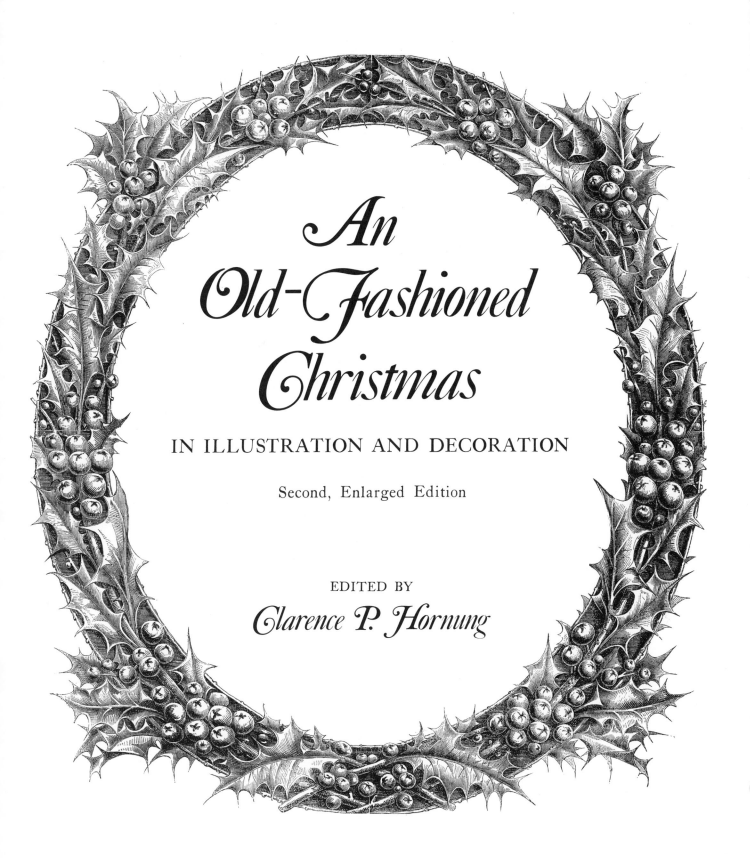

An Old-Fashioned Christmas

IN ILLUSTRATION AND DECORATION

Second, Enlarged Edition

EDITED BY

Clarence P. Hornung

DOVER PUBLICATIONS, INC., NEW YORK

Published in Canada by General Publishing Company, Ltd., 30 Lesmill Road, Don Mills, Toronto, Ontario.

Published in the United Kingdom by Constable and Company, Ltd., 10 Orange Street, London WC 2.

An Old-Fashioned Christmas in Illustration and Decoration, published in 1975, is an enlarged edition of the work first published by Dover Publications, Inc., in 1970.

DOVER *Pictorial Archive* SERIES

International Standard Book Number: 0-486-22367-1
Library of Congress Catalog Card Number: 71-138389

Manufactured in the United States of America
Dover Publications, Inc.
180 Varick Street
New York, N.Y. 10014

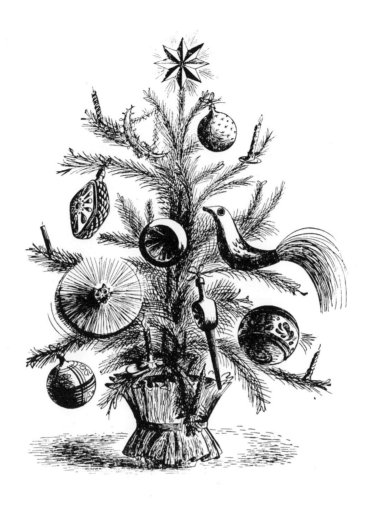

EDITOR'S NOTE

"Christmas comes but once a year"—so I was admonished as a child. But when I became an artist I learned that to my profession it comes a second time: during the hot summer days when the commercial artist and illustrator "celebrates" Christmas at his drawing board, working on greeting cards, gift catalogs, advertisements. I compiled this book to make the artist's Christmas a little easier. Here are the picture resources to get the job done a little better and faster. "Yes, Virginia, there is a Santa Claus"—but he is Tom Nast's Santa Claus and the artist is well advised to have this Santa before him on holiday assignments. In addition to many Nast drawings, I have gathered pictures and decorations depicting the fun, good fellowship and lore of Christmas. There are numerous charming winter scenes —skating, snow-ball fights, sleighing—Christmas trees and gay decorations, dances under the mistletoe, gift giving, caroling, Christmas Eve, Christmas Day. The illustrations have been arranged to correspond with the sequence of events at Christmas: from bringing home the Christmas tree to the festive Christmas dinner.

The iconography of the nonreligious aspects of Christmas is scarce and recent. The very first Christmas card, pictured on the back cover through the courtesy of the Hallmark Historical Collection, appeared in 1843. My grandfather might have received it! Most of the artists who created the visual images of Christmas were alive in the recent past: Walter Crane, Randolph Caldecott and Tom Nast. I've tried to represent all of them and other artists now unknown but whose work is redolent of Christmases past.

It is interesting that despite so many radical shifts in public taste, the symbols and pictures of old Christmas have not been affected and can be used without ambiguity and without offense. I have deliberately excluded all religious aspects of Christmas. This is the subject of a more serious, reverent work devoid of the commercial intent of this volume.

Wherever possible I have given the source of each illustration. The material was collected over a period of years and I regret that in a few instances I lost track of the sources. I am grateful to Walter Schatzki for his advice. Mr. and Mrs. Sherman P. Haight and Mr. Leslie Dorsey were kind enough to let me use their excellent collections. As always, Romana Javitz of the New York Public Library Picture Collection was most helpful. Thanks also to Photo Lettering, Inc., 216 East 45th Street, New York City 10036, a typographic firm which supplied the appropriate sentiments found on pages 112 and 113, and which is equipped to prepare on order longer messages in any of the special typefaces shown. I relied upon the knowledgeable help of John Grafton, Clarence Strowbridge and the Dover staff, and I was encouraged by Hayward Cirker's enthusiasm to bring the project to completion.

In typical commercial-artist fashion, I have completed this Christmas book in midsummer. I send greetings to all artists similarly engaged and hope that in spite of having to suffer through the sultry dog-days of July and August, their deep involvement on the Christmas theme will be a harbinger of the time of snow flakes, tinsel and mistletoe.

CLARENCE P. HORNUNG

July, 1970

To make *An Old-fashioned Christmas* more useful, an additional thirty-two pages have been added to this edition. None of the illustrations of the first edition has been omitted. Some, formerly on one page, are now reproduced on double-page spreads. Among the many new illustrations are additional works by Nast, Tenniel and the other artists of the nineteenth century who helped to create the iconography of Christmas.

1975   C. H.

"The Old Homestead—Going Home for the Holidays," by Granville Perkins.
From *Harper's Weekly*, Dec. 25, 1875.

"Getting Ready for Christmas," by W. L. Sheppard, *c.* 1882.

"The Time When We Were Boys," by T. S. Church. From *Harper's Weekly*,
Jan. 11, 1873.

From *St. Nicholas* Magazine, *c.* 1882.

"ON CHRISTMAS DAY IN THE MORNING"
WITH THE COMPLIMENTS OF ST. NICHOLAS

From *St. Nicholas* Magazine, Dec., 1882.

Christmas, 1860.

A happy Christmas-tide to ev'ry one!
Though from the festal board some
    guests are gone.
And yet not gone, for to each vacant place
There cometh one who hath an angel's
    face!
And there is left a store of life and love,
Links which unite us here to those above.

A happy Christmas-tide! And let the
    poor
Turn with a thankful heart from ev'ry
    door.
If in our hearts there's strife with kin
    or friend,
For Jesu's sake, let the contention end.
So, ere the year is hidden 'neath its
    pall,
Thank we the Lord, to be at peace with
    all.

From *Illustrated London News*, Dec. 22, 1860.

"Christmas in France," by F. Méaulle, 1875.

"Christmas." From *Godey's Lady's Book and Magazine*, Dec., 1869.

"Winter Sports—Coasting in the Country," by Granville Perkins.
From *Harper's Weekly,* Feb. 17, 1877.

"The Snow Battle." From *Harper's Weekly, c.* 1872.

"The Snow-Ball of the Season," by Alfred Fredericks. From *Harper's Weekly, c.* 1871.

"A Snow Scene on Boston Common."
From *Ballou's Pictorial Drawingroom Companion*, 1856.

"The First Snow-Ball."

"Trotters on the Snow," by Thomas Worth. From *Harper's Weekly*, Jan. 23, 1869.

15

Illustration by J. P. Davis. From *Santa Claus on a Lark* by Washington Gladden, 1890.

"Christmas Belles," by Winslow Homer. From *Harper's Weekly*, Jan. 2, 1869.

"Skating at Boston." From *Harper's Weekly*, March 12, 1859.

"Skating Season—1862." From *Harper's Weekly*, Jan. 18, 1862.

"Christmas Out of Doors."
From *Harper's Weekly*, Dec. 25, 1858.

"Oatman's Fifth Avenue Skating Rink—First Lesson in Skating."
From *Harper's Weekly*, Jan. 12, 1867.

"Christmas Decorations by Jack Frost."
From *Frank Leslie's Illustrated Newspaper, c.* 1885.

"A Christmas Welcome," by Edward Hughes.
From *Illustrated London News* (Christmas Supplement), Dec. 16, 1871.

23

"Christmas of the Present, 1859," by Macquoid.
From *Illustrated London News,* Dec. 31, 1859.

"Preparing Christmas Greens," by T. De Thulstrup.
From *Harper's Weekly*, Dec. 25, 1880.

"Selling Christmas Greens—A Scene in Richmond, Virginia," by W. L. Sheppard.
From *Harper's Weekly,* Dec. 25, 1875.

"Bringing Home the Christmas Tree," by Alfred Hunt.
From *Illustrated London News,* 1882.

27

"The Mistletoe Seller," by B. Foster. From *Illustrated London News*, Dec. 23, 1854.

"The Mistletoe Seller," by Phiz. From *Illustrated London News*, Dec. 24, 1853.

"Gathering Christmas Greens." An illustration from *c.* 1876.

Top: An illustration from *The Fir Tree* by Hans Christian Andersen, 1850.
Bottom: Illustration by Ludwig Richter, c. 1803.

From *Punch*, 1847.

The Dear Old Tree

BY LUELLA WILSON SMITH

There's a
dear old tree,
an evergreen
tree,
And it blossoms
once a year.
'Tis loaded
with fruit from
top to root,
And it brings to
all good cheer.

For its blossoms
bright are small
candles white
And its fruit is
dolls and toys.
And they all are
free for both
you and me
If we're good little
girls & boys.

From *St. Nicholas* Magazine, Dec., 1907.

Three decorated Christmas trees from turn-of-the-century magazines.

"Hoisting the Union Jack," by Alfred Hunt. From *Illustrated London News,* Dec., 1876.

"The Christmas Tree," by F. A. Chapman.

"Christmas Games."
From *Godey's Lady's Book and Magazine*, Dec., 1869.

"Santa Claus Is Coming !," by Thomas Worth. From *Harper's Weekly,* Dec. 26, 1874.

"Santa Claus in the Act of Descending a Chimney on Christmas Eve."
From *The Great Pictorial Annual Brother Jonathan*, Jan. 1, 1845.

"A Visit from St. Nicholas," Thomas Nast's first published Santa Claus picture.
From *Christmas Poems*, 1863-64.

Illustration by Thomas Nast.
From *Harper's Weekly* (Christmas Supplement), Dec. 31, 1870.

"Seeing Santa Claus," by Thomas Nast. From *Harper's Weekly* (Supplement),
Jan. 1, 1876.

"Merry Christmas," by Thomas Nast. From *Harper's Weekly*, Jan. 4, 1879.

A famous Christmas picture by Thomas Nast from *Harper's Weekly*, Dec. 29, 1866. A detail is shown on the opposite page.

"Santa Claus's Mail," by Thomas Nast.
From *Harper's Weekly,* Dec. 30, 1871.

"Merry Old Santa Claus," by Thomas Nast. From *Harper's Weekly*, Jan. 1, 1881.

47

"The Watch on Christmas-Eve," by Thomas Nast. From *Harper's Weekly*, Jan. 1, 1876.

"A Chance to Test Santa Claus's Generosity," by Thomas Nast.
From *Harper's Weekly*, Dec. 30, 1876.

"Santa Claus Can't Say That I've Forgotten Anything," by Thomas Nast.
From *Harper's Weekly*, Dec. 25, 1886.

"Not a Creature Was Stirring, *Not Even a Mouse*," by Thomas Nast.
From *Harper's Weekly*, Dec. 25, 1886.

"Another Stocking to Fill," by Thomas Nast. From *Harper's Weekly*, Jan. 3, 1880.

"Christmas, 1863," by Thomas Nast. From *Harper's Weekly*, Dec. 26, 1863.

"Christmas Post," by Thomas Nast. From *Harper's Weekly,* Jan. 4, 1879.

"The Dear Little Boy That Thought Christmas Came Oftener," by Thomas Nast.
From *Harper's Weekly,* Jan. 1, 1881.

"Caught!," by Thomas Nast. From *Harper's Weekly*, Dec. 24, 1881.

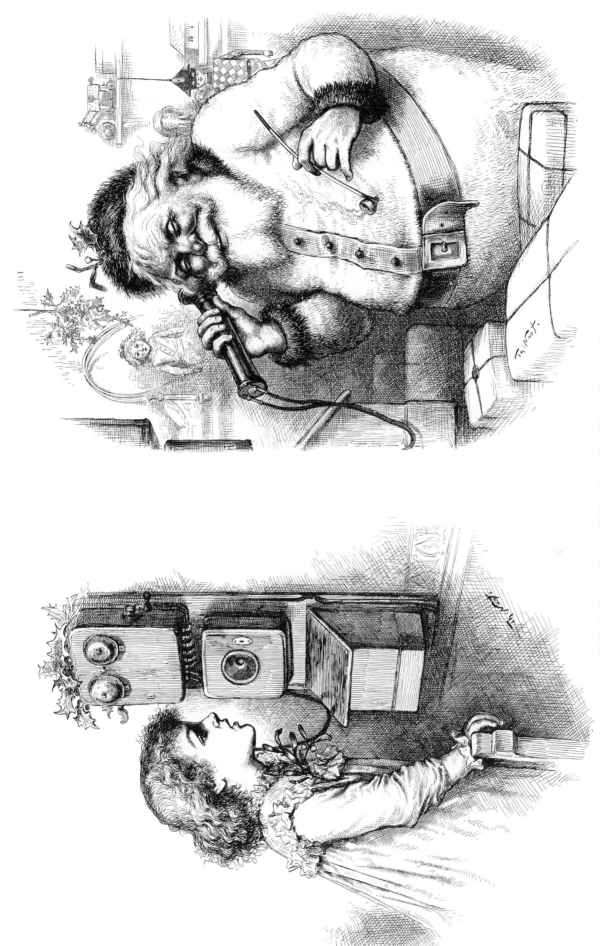

" 'Hello, Santa Claus!' 'Hello, Little One!' " By Thomas Nast,
from *Harper's Weekly*, Dec. 20, 1884.

"The Coming of Santa Claus," by Thomas Nast, 1872.

"Santa Claus," by Charles G. Bush. From *Harper's Weekly*, Dec. 28, 1867.

Illustration from *Santa Claus on a Lark* by Washington Gladden, 1890.

"Childhood's Faith in Santa Claus—The Christmas Letter."
From *Frank Leslie's Illustrated Newspaper*, 1887.

61

"Santa Claus and His Presents." From *Harper's Weekly*, Dec. 25, 1858.

"The Christmas Dream," by Jules Taverner.
From *Harper's Weekly* (Supplement), Dec. 30, 1871.

Illustration by R. F. Bunner from *Santa Claus on a Lark*
by Washington Gladden, 1890.

"Merry Christmas," by Kenny Meadows. From *Illustrated London News, c.* 1865.

Illustration by John Leech from *A Christmas Carol* by Charles Dickens, 1843.

"Christmas Pleasures and Annoyances," by W. McConnell.
From *Illustrated London Times*, Dec. 20, 1856.

A picture by Boudeville from *L'Illustration*, Dec. 25, 1858.

"Uncle John with the Young Folk: All Prizes and No Blanks!"
A picture by A. B. Houghton from *Illustrated London News*, Dec. 23, 1865.

"The Christmas Tree," by J. A. Pasquier. From *Illustrated London News*, Dec. 25, 1858.

73

"A Christmas Party. Grandpa Dances 'Sir Roger,' and
May He Dance It for Many, Many Years to Come!" From *Punch*, 1856.

"The Last Night of the Mistletoe," by J. Godwin.
From *Illustrated London News*, Dec. 24, 1859.

"COLD CHRISTMAS?—NO!."

From *Illustrated London News,* Dec. 24, 1853.

"The Christmas-Tree," by Winslow Homer. From *Harper's Weekly*, Dec. 25, 1858.

"The Children's Party—After Supper," by F. W. Lawson.
From *The Graphic* (Christmas Number), Dec. 25, 1873.

"Uncle William's Christmas Presents," by John Gilbert.
From *Illustrated London News*, Dec. 20, 1856.

"Christmas a Long Time Ago." From *London Illustrated Times*, Dec. 20, 1856.

Half-title page from *Punch*, 1855.

"Hurrah for the Pudding!" From *Little Folks, c.* 1870.

"New England Christmas Home Scenes, and Christmas Games."
From *Ballou's Pictorial Drawingroom Companion*, Dec. 24, 1853.

"Burning the Christmas Greens." From *Harper's Weekly*, 1876.

"Under the Mistletoe." From an engraving dated 1868.

"Doll-Makers and Doll-Breakers." From *Harper's Weekly* (Christmas Supplement), Dec. 28, 1878.

86

"An Early Christmas Call." From *Harper's Weekly*, Dec. 28, 1867.

"Faith—Waiting for Santa Claus," by M. Woolf. From *Harper's Weekly*, Dec. 26, 1874.

"The Children's Corner at the Centennial—Exhibition of Dolls and Toys," by Theodore R. Davis, 1877.

This page and the next six show Christmas gift toys from
Marshall Field and Company's *Illustrated Catalogue,* Chicago, 1891-92.

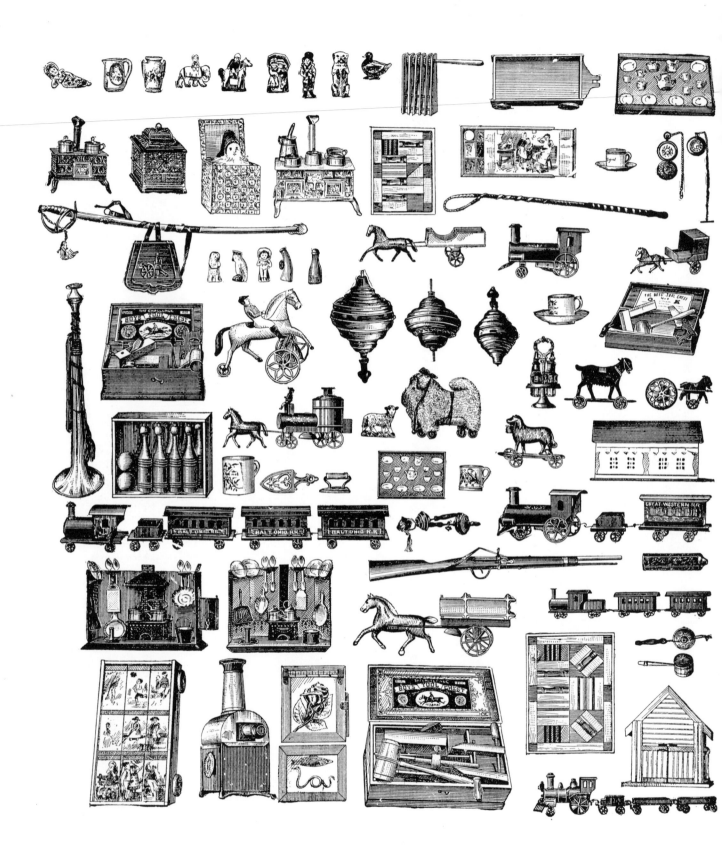

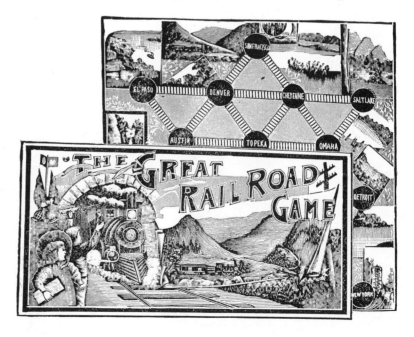

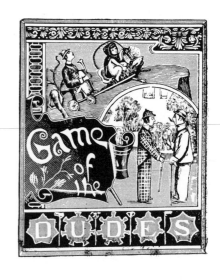

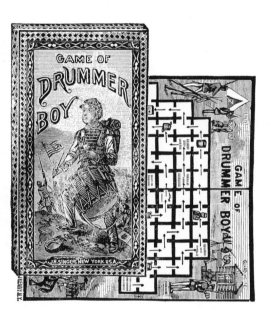

PROFESSOR PUG FROGS GREAT BICYCLE FEAT

A.MUCFORD HFD.CT.

Illustrations by Randolph Caldecott.
From *Old Christmas, from the Sketch Book of Washington Irving*, 1875.

Twelve illustrations by Randolph Caldecott.
From *Old Christmas, from the Sketch Book of Washington Irving*, 1875.

Illustration by Randolph Caldecott.

From *Old Christmas, from the Sketch Book of Washington Irving*, 1875.

The bottom shows an early Christmas card by W. M. Egley, 1848.

At left: "Bringing in the Boar's Head." From *Harper's Monthly,* Jan., 1873.

From *St. Nicholas* Magazine, *c.* 1896.

From *St. Nicholas* Magazine, *c.* 1895.

The Story of the Holly Sprig

BY ARTHUR UPSON

"I 'D be the shiniest green,"
  Wished once a sprig of holly,
"That e'er at Yule was seen,
  And deck some banquet jolly!"

"I 'd be the cheeriest red,"
  Wished once the holly-berry,
"That e'er at board rich spread
  Helped make the feasters merry!"

The life within them heard
  Down dark and silent courses,
For each wish is a word
  To those fair-hidden sources.

All Summer in the wood,
  While they were riper growing,
The deep roots understood,
  And helped without their knowing.

In a little market stall
  At Yule the sprig lay waiting,
For fine folk one and all
  Passed by that open grating.

The Eve of Christmas Day
  It had been passed by many,
When one turned not away
  And bought it for a penny.

Hers was a home of care
  Which not a wreath made jolly;
The only Christmas there
  Was that sweet sprig of holly.

"Oh, this is better far
  Than banquet!" thought the berry;
The leaves glowed like a star
  And made that cottage merry!

From *St. Nicholas* Magazine, *c.* 1907.

At the Sign of the Christmas Tree

Ho, for the ancient hostelry,
Whose generous doors swing wide and free!
Whose guests, when the first snow crystals fall,
Gather within its spacious hall
From north and from south, and from west to east,
Big folks down to the very least,
Thronging, far as the eye can see,
To lodge at The Sign of the Christmas Tree.

The guests are known by their curious wiles,
Mysterious nods, and becks, and smiles;
There are secrets flying about by scores,
Smothered laughs behind fast-closed doors;
There's a noise of hammers, and tink of bells,
And whispered "Hushes," and soft "Don't tells."
Oh, a wonderful place for mystery
Is the ancient Inn of the Christmas Tree!

There guests sit apart, and stitch and sew
On woven linen as white as snow;
Flowers bloom bright on silken fields,
And fresh surprises each moment yields.
And the room where they sit is like a dream,
Where scarlet berries of holly gleam;

A double-page illustration from *St. Nicholas* Magazine, *c.* 1908.

By Pauline Frances Camp

And over the lintel, in gold, is wrought
Its beautiful name of "Loving Thought."

And Peggy, and Polly, and Pete, and Prue,
With a dear little girl that looks like you,
A red-haired lass, and a blue-eyed lad,
Grandmother dear, and Mother, and Dad,
And hundreds of others all over the land,
Are working away with heart and hand,
Snipping and clipping, where none may see,
At the Merry Sign of the Christmas Tree.

But oh, dear people who long have been
Guests 'neath the roof of this pleasant inn,
Bethink, there are those who do not belong
To the work and fun, to the cheer and song!
Empty-handed and wistful-eyed,
They are out in the cold this Christmas-tide.
Tie up your parcels with ribbon gay;
Sprig them with green in the good old way;
Then, from your riches, where need is seen
Fill up the lives that are bare and lean.
So shall a gracious blessing be
Called down on The Sign of the Christmas Tree!

Christmas·Merrymaking

Caput·apri·defero

S·Stephen·

Five illustrations by Walter Crane from *A Book of Christmas Verse*,
selected by H. C. Beeching, 1895.

The Angels

Ceremonies for Christmas

"Christmas Bells," by Lorenz Frölich.
From *Illustrated London News*, Dec. 21, 1872

"King Cheer," by James Godwin.
From *Illustrated London News*, Dec. 24, 1864.

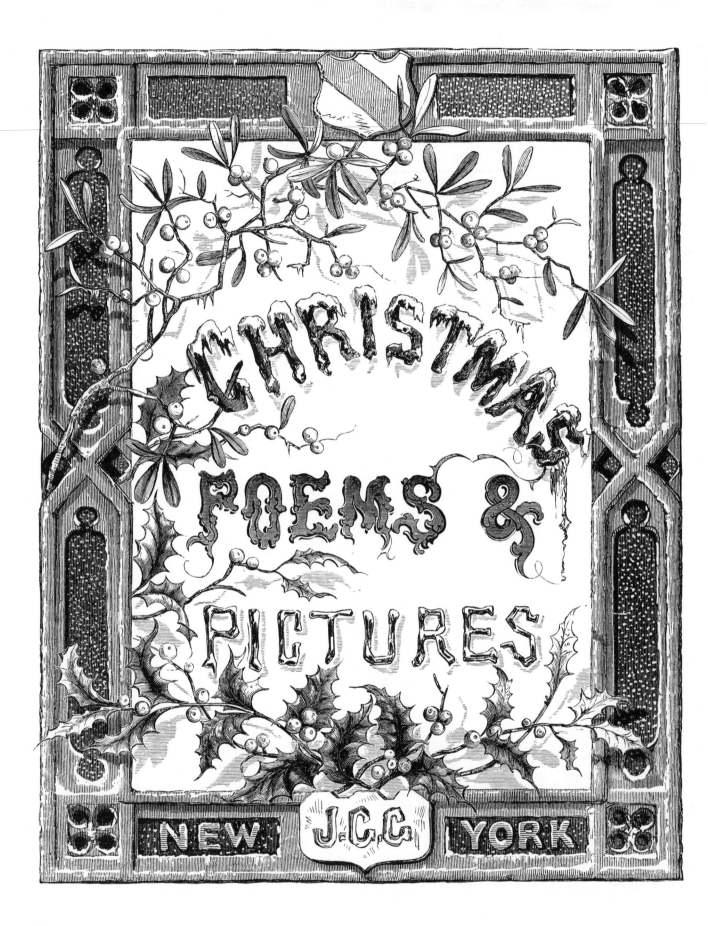

"Christmas for Ever!"

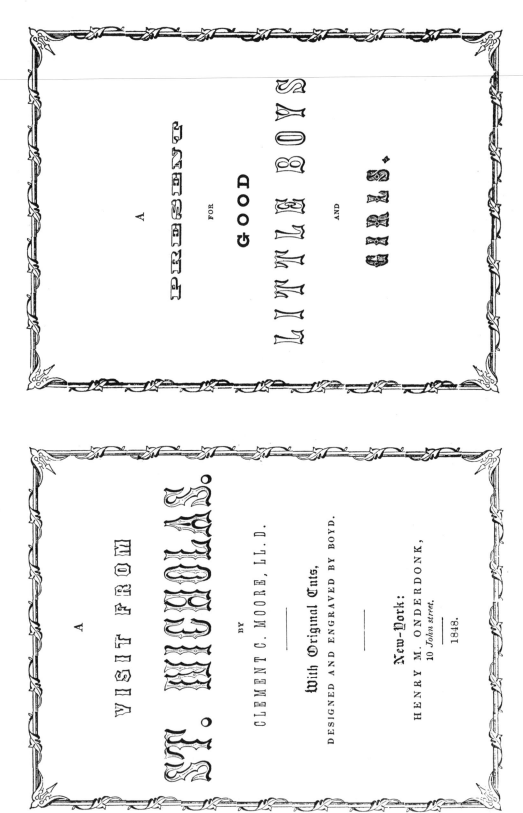

A PRESENT FOR GOOD LITTLE BOYS AND GIRLS.

A VISIT FROM ST. NICHOLAS.

BY

CLEMENT C. MOORE, LL. D.

With Original Cuts,

DESIGNED AND ENGRAVED BY BOYD.

New-York:

HENRY M. ONDERDONK,
10 John street.

1848.

A complete facsimile of the first illustrated edition of *The Night Before Christmas.* (pages 84-90)

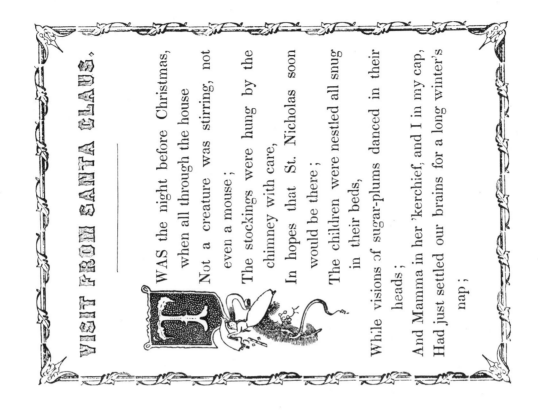

VISIT FROM SANTA CLAUS.

WAS the night before Christmas,
when all through the house
Not a creature was stirring, not
even a mouse;
The stockings were hung by the
chimney with care,
In hopes that St. Nicholas soon
would be there;
The children were nestled all snug
in their beds,
While visions of sugar-plums danced in their
heads;
And Mamma in her 'kerchief, and I in my cap,
Had just settled our brains for a long winter's
nap;

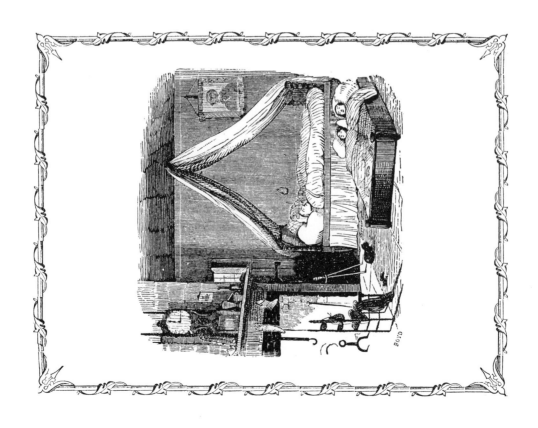

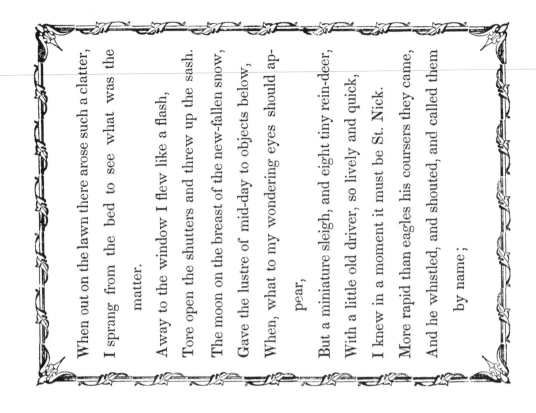

When out on the lawn there arose such a clatter,
I sprang from the bed to see what was the
	matter.
Away to the window I flew like a flash,
Tore open the shutters and threw up the sash.
The moon on the breast of the new-fallen snow,
Gave the lustre of mid-day to objects below,
When, what to my wondering eyes should ap-
	pear,
But a miniature sleigh, and eight tiny rein-deer,
With a little old driver, so lively and quick,
I knew in a moment it must be St. Nick.
More rapid than eagles his coursers they came,
And he whistled, and shouted, and called them
	by name ;

"Now, *Dasher!* now, *Dancer!* now, *Prancer*
and *Vixen!*

On, *Comet!* on, *Cupid!* on, *Donder* and *Blitzen!*

To the top of the porch! to the top of the
wall!

Now dash away! dash away! dash away
all!"

As dry leaves that before the wild hurricane
fly,

When they meet with an obstacle, mount to
the sky;

So up to the house-top the coursers they flew,
With the sleigh full of Toys, and St. Nicholas
too.

And then in a twinkling, I heard on the roof,
The prancing and pawing of each little hoof —

As I drew in my head, and was turning around,

Down the chimney St. Nicholas came with a bound.

He was dressed all in fur, from his head to his foot,

And his clothes were all tarnished with ashes and soot;

A bundle of Toys he had flung on his back,

And he looked like a pedlar just opening his pack.

His eyes—how they twinkled! his dimples, how merry!

His cheeks were like roses, his nose like a cherry!

His droll little mouth was drawn up like a bow,

And the beard of his chin was as white as the snow;

The stump of a pipe he held tight in his teeth,

And the smoke it encircled his head like a
    wreath ;

He had a broad face and a little round belly,

That shook when he laughed, like a bowlfull
    of jelly.

He was chubby and plump, a right jolly old elf,

And I laughed when I saw him, in spite of
    myself,

A wink of his eye and a twist of his head,

Soon gave me to know I had nothing to dread ;

He spoke not a word, but went straight to his
    work,

And fill'd all the stockings ; then turned with a
    jerk,

And laying his finger aside of his nose,

And giving a nod, up the chimney he rose;

He sprang to his sleigh, to his team gave a whistle,

And away they all flew like the down of a thistle.

But I heard him exclaim, ere he drove out of sight,

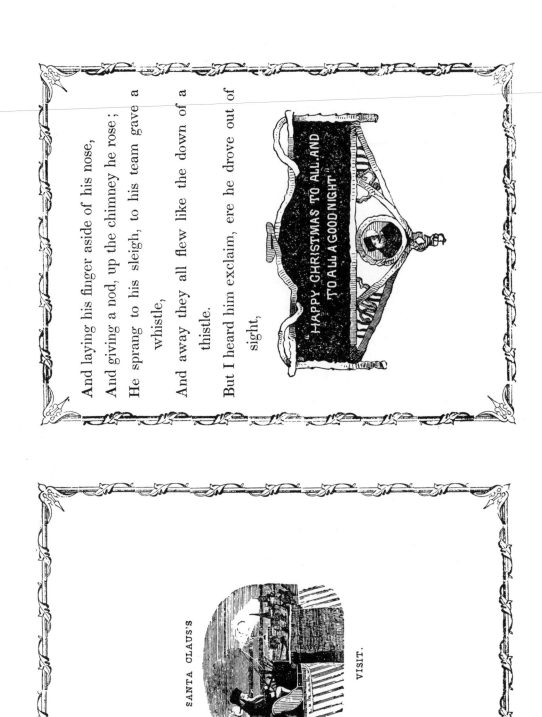

HAPPY CHRISTMAS TO ALL, AND TO ALL A GOOD NIGHT.

SANTA CLAUS'S

VISIT.

The title page, followed by a selection of eight pages in facsimile, from *The Night Before Christmas* by Clement Moore as published by Porter and Coats in Philadelphia in 1883. The illustrations are by William T. Smedley, Frederick B. Schell, Alfred Fredericks and Henry R. Poore.

WITH a little old driver, so lively and quick,
I knew in a moment it must be St. Nick.

MORE rapid than eagles his coursers they came,
    And he whistled and shouted and called them by name:
"Now Dasher! now Dancer! now Prancer! now Vixen!
On, Comet! on, Cupid! on, Donder and Blitzen!

"TO the top of
the porch!
To the top of
the wall!

Now,
dash away,
dash away, dash
away, all!"
As dry leaves that before
the wild hurricane fly,
When they meet with
an obstacle,
mount to
the sky,

So up to the
housetop the
coursers they flew,
With the sleigh full of toys and St. Nicholas too.
And then, in a twinkling, I heard on the roof
The prancing and pawing of each little hoof.

HIS eyes: how they twinkled! his dimples: how merry!
His cheeks were like roses, his nose like a cherry;

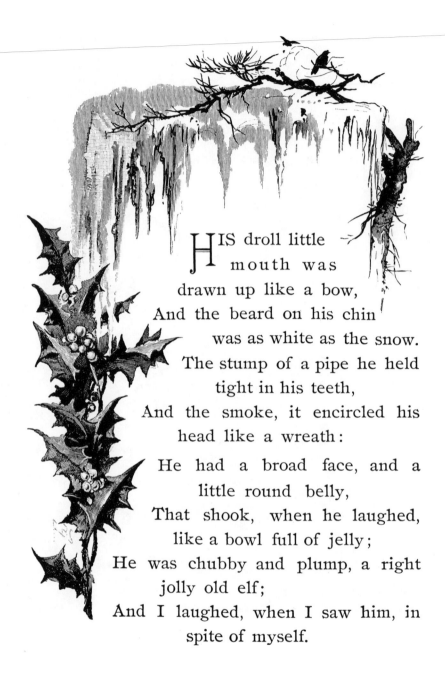

HIS droll little
mouth was
drawn up like a bow,
And the beard on his chin
was as white as the snow.
The stump of a pipe he held
tight in his teeth,
And the smoke, it encircled his
head like a wreath:

He had a broad face, and a
little round belly,
That shook, when he laughed,
like a bowl full of jelly;
He was chubby and plump, a right
jolly old elf;
And I laughed, when I saw him, in
spite of myself.

HE sprang to his sleigh, to his team gave
     a whistle,
And away they all flew like the down of
     a thistle;

A double-page illustration by Louis Rhead from *St. Nicholas* Magazine, *c.* 1893.

III.

I tossed them holly in hall and cot,
 And bade them right good cheer,
But ·stayed me not in any spot,
 For I 'd traveled around the year

IV.

To bring the Christmas joy, my dears,
 To your eyes so bonnie and true ;
And a mistletoe bough for you, my dears,
 A mistletoe bough for you !

bring the Christmas joy, my dears, To your eyes so bonnie and true ; And a

(For music complete, with words, see page 188.)

mistle-toe bough for you, my dears, A mis-tle-toe bough for you!

A series of nine illustrations from *St. Nicholas* Magazine, *c.* 1905.

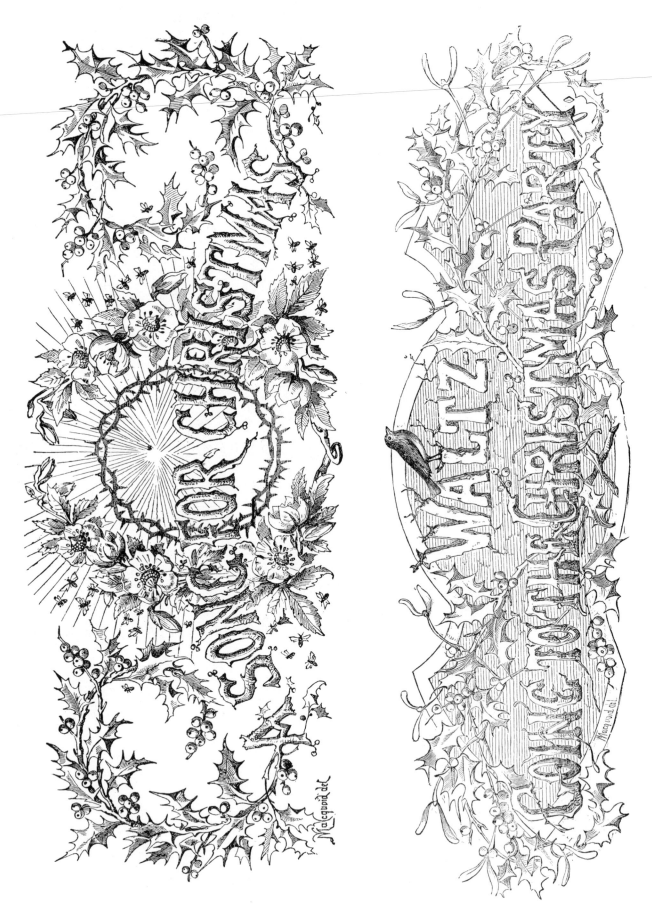

Illustrations by Macquoid from *Illustrated London News.* The one at the top dates from Dec. 19, 1857 ; the other from Dec. 24, 1859.

Holly-leaf motif typographic ornaments from a turn-of-the-century catalog
of the American Type Founders Company.

Four pages of snow flakes selected from *Cloud Crystals, A Snow Flake Album,* collected and edited by "A Lady," and published by D. Appleton in New York in 1864.

A decorative alphabet executed with logs and greens.

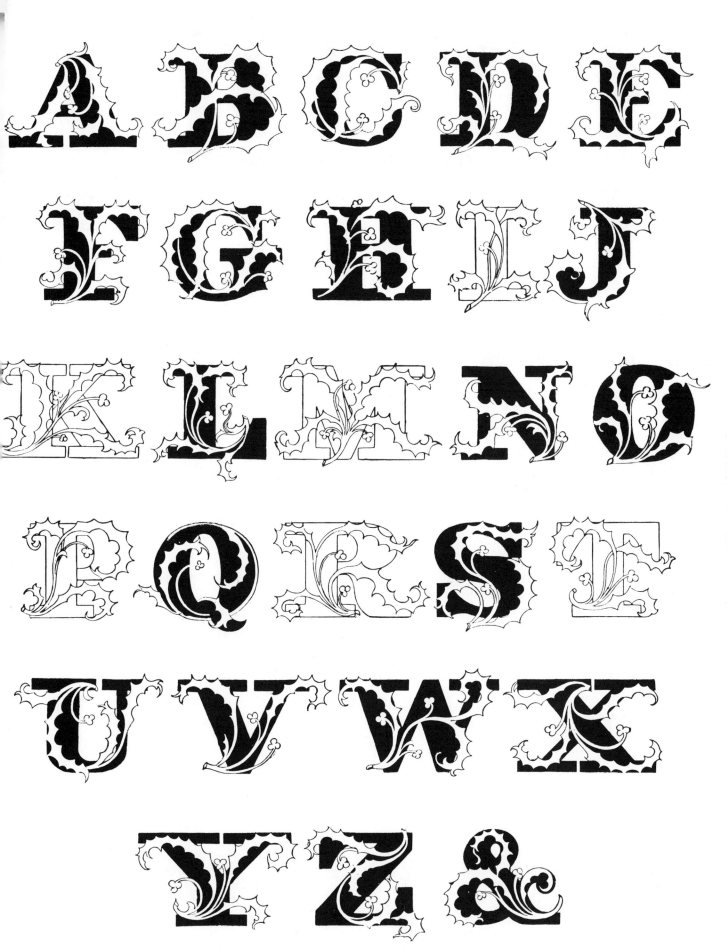

An alphabet based on the holly-leaf motif.

MERRY CHRISTMAS

MERRY CHRISTMAS

MERRY CHRISTMAS

MERRY CHRISTMAS

MERRY CHRISTMAS

MERRY CHRISTMAS

MERRY CHRISTMAS

142 The greetings on these two pages were prepared in unusual typefaces appropriate to
the Christmas season specially for the present publication by Photo Lettering, Inc. in New York City.

SEASON'S GREETINGS

SEASON'S GREETINGS

SEASON'S GREETINGS

SEASON'S GREETINGS

SEASON'S GREETINGS

SEASON'S GREETINGS

SEASON'S GREETINGS

WET, BUT WELCOME.

Mrs. Bull. "LA! FATHER CHRISTMAS, YOU'VE ONLY TO GET INTO YOUR DRY CLOTHES, AND TAKE PLENTY OF *THIS*, AND YOU'LL BE MERRY ENOUGH, I WARRANT!"

Illustration by John Tenniel. From *Punch*, Dec. 28, 1872.

CHRISTMAS À LA MODE.

FATHER CHRISTMAS. "CONCRETE AND WHEEL-SKATES! THAT I SHOULD EVER COME TO THIS! HE! HE! REALLY, THOUGH, I RATHER LIKE IT!!"

Illustration by John Tenniel. From *Punch,* Dec. 25, 1875.

AN ARDUOUS QUEST.

Mr. Punch. "WHAT ARE YOU LOOKING FOR, FATHER?"
Father Christmas. "PEACE ON EARTH, AND GOODWILL TOWARDS MEN!"

Illustration by John Tenniel. From *Punch*, Dec. 28, 1878.

STRANGERS.

FATHER CHRISTMAS. "WHAT! NOT KNOW *ME*!—OH, THIS MUST BE ALTERED!"

Illustration by John Tenniel. From *Punch*, Dec. 29, 1883.

THE WASSAIL BOWL.

"DROP PARTY SPIRIT QUITE,
  'TIS HEAVY, HEADY, STUFF,
ALL MEN *PUNCH* DOTH INVITE
  TO TIPPLE *QUANTUM SUFF*:
     OF HIS WASSAIL!

"GOOD LUCK BETIDE YOU ALL!
  ONE BUMPER MORE WE'LL FILL;
PUNCH HOPES, AND EVER SHALL,
  FOR PEACE AND FOR GOOD-WILL.
     THAT'S HIS WASSAIL!"

      Illustration by John Tenniel. From *Punch*, Dec. 29, 1888.

A CHRISTMAS PUZZLE.

FATHER CHRISTMAS. "NOW, MY LITTLE MAN, WHERE'S YOUR *STOCKING?*"
POOR LITTLE WAIF. "PLEASE, SIR, I AIN'T GOT NE'ER A ONE!"

Illustration by John Tenniel. From *Punch,* Dec 28, 1895.

FATHER CHRISTMAS—"UP-TO-DATE."

Illustration by John Tenniel. From *Punch,* Dec 26, 1896.

TO "ABSENT FRIENDS!"

Illustration by John Tenniel. From *Punch*, Dec. 26, 1900.

PART 1st TURKEY
INVITED OUT TO DINE.

2nd SKIRMISHING
AGAINST TURKEY.

DINING ROOM

SANTA CLAUS.
I AM JUST IN TIME
FOR DINNER.

WELCOME ALL TO DINNER

DINNER   DINNER

THE DREA

5th TURKEYS GUESTS.

"A Dream of a Christmas Dinner, in Five Parts," by Thomas Worth. From *Harper's Weekly*, Dec. 26, 1874.